Nature's Children

PIGS

by Maggie da Silva

Grolier Educational

FACTS IN BRIEF

Classification of the Pig

Class:	*Mammalia* (mammals)
Order:	*Artiodactyla* (even-toed hoofed animals)
Suborder:	*Swine*
Family:	*Suidae*
SubFamily:	*Suinae*
Genus:	*Sus*
Species:	*S. scrofa*

World Distribution. Domestic pigs are produced in large numbers throughout most of the world.

Habitat. Some domestic pigs graze on pastures while most other pigs are kept in either small, clean sheds or pens.

Distinctive physical characteristics. Plump, medium-sized body covered with coarse hair, large head, strong, moveable snout, short tail, and teeth that grow outward and upward like tusks.

Habits. Pigs have a keen sense of smell and use their snouts to root in the ground for food. They are good swimmers and can also trot, canter, and run fast. Pigs wallow in mud to protect themselves from the hot sun.

Diet. Corn, grain, barley, wheat, rye, oats, commercial feeds, and edible garbage.

Library of Congress Cataloging-in-Publication Data

Weil, Ann. 1960-
    Pigs / Ann Weil.
        p.   cm. — (Nature's children)
    Includes index.
    Summary: Describes the physical characteristics, behavior
distribution, and care of pigs.
    ISBN 0-7172-9073-5 (hardbound)
    1. Swine—Juvenile literature.   [1. Pigs.]   I. Title.
II. Series.
SF395.5.W45 1997
636.4—dc21

97-5971
CIP
AC

This library reinforced edition was published in 1997 exclusively by:

 Grolier Educational

Sherman Turnpike, Danbury, Connecticut 06816

Set ISBN 0-7172-7661-9
Pigs ISBN 0-7172-9073-5

Contents

Relatives and Ancestors — Page 6

What a Boar — Page 9

Pigs and People — Page 10

Some Pig! — Page 12

Life on the Farm — Page 15

Only the Squeal Is Left — Page 16

The Pig Sty — Page 18

Types of Pigs — Page 19

A Colorful Cast of Characters — Page 20

Pigs and Medicine — Page 22

Vietnamese Pot-Bellied Pigs — Page 23

Apartment Wanted . . . Maybe — Page 24

Keeping a Pet Pig — Page 27

Supplies and Equipment — Page 28

Being a Responsible Owner — Page 31

Diet and Nutrition — Page 32

Handling — Page 35

Health Care — Page 36

Pig Behavior — Page 39

Getting Along with Others — Page 40

Why Neuter Pigs? — Page 43

Here Come the Piglets — Page 44

Famous Pigs — Page 46

Words to Know — Page 47

Index — Page 48

*For many people pigs have an
appeal all their own.*

To most people pigs are fat, pink animals that live on farms and like to play in the mud. But there is more to pigs than this.

To begin with, pigs come in many different colors, shapes, and sizes. They live all over the world and in some places even run wild. And although pigs do like mud, they actually are one of the cleanest animals around.

Like people, pigs are mammals. This means that baby pigs are born alive, not in eggs. It also means that female pigs produce milk to feed their young.

Unlike humans, however, pigs have four toes on each foot, and their stomachs have two chambers. Pigs also have a snout instead of a nose. This snout is a remarkable tool that can move in all different directions. It even has a strong tip at the end that pigs use for rooting in the dirt.

Most pigs are raised on farms for their meat. However, pigs are such intelligent, interesting animals that some people just can't resist keeping them as pets.

Relatives and Ancestors

The domestic, or tame, pig is a member of a family of animals called Suidae, which is part of the order Artiodactyla. Other Artiodactyla include cattle, deer, and peccaries. (Peccaries look like slim versions of pigs and are the closest living relatives of the domestic pig.) All Artiodactyla have hooves and an even number of toes on each foot.

The earliest ancestor of the pig appeared in Asia about 65 million years ago. Pigs are also known to have been in Africa about 25 million years ago. The wild boar, the domestic pig's closest relative, developed about 5 million years ago. Ancient cave paintings show early humans hunting these wild pigs.

About 8,000 years ago people in Asia and Europe started to tame and raise pigs. After 1493, when Christopher Columbus brought pigs to the West Indies, they spread to the Americas. Other European explorers and settlers brought pigs as well. Soon North, Central, and South America had both wild and domestic pigs, too.

Some people find pigs so cute that they take them in as pets.

Domestic pigs tend to come in the giant economy size—as long as six feet (1.8 meters) and as heavy as 600 pounds (270 kilograms) or more.

What a Boar

Although all adult male pigs are called boars, the word also is used to describe wild pigs. These creatures look little like their domestic relatives, and they are known for their fierce behavior.

Today wild boars wander the forests of Europe and Asia as well as the plains of South Africa. They come in many sizes and colors, from the tiny pygmy hog of Nepal, Bhutan, and northern India to the giant African forest hog. The biggest of all pigs, it can be as much as six and half feet (2 meters) long, and three and half feet (1 meter) tall, and more then 600 pounds (270 kilograms)! The Eurasian wild boar is sometimes just as enormous, six feet (1.8 meters) long and three feet (91.4 centimeters) tall.

These may be big pigs, but they are nothing compared with the warthog, the fiercest looking pig of all. It has large tusks that curve outward and upward, and the males have two pairs of rough, warty outgrowths on their faces.

Pigs and People

Today pigs are raised mainly for meat. But the animal has had many different uses over the ages.

In ancient Egypt, for example, people used pigs to help plant the fields. It seems that when pigs walked, they made holes in the ground that were just the right size for seeds. In time the Egyptians trained their pigs to put holes in just the right places for the seeds.

The Romans had a different but equally important job for their pigs. The people of ancient Rome believed that if they swore an oath on a pig, that oath was more serious. So promising or saying something on a pig was a sign of truth and trust.

In other places pigs had the kinds of jobs we normally give to dogs. For example, in England people actually had hunting pigs. These pigs pointed out game and fetched it after it had been killed. And in India people found that pigs could be used to take care of other animals. According to experts, Indian pigs were used to herd buffalo!

At various times, pigs have been used
to plant seeds, hunt for wild game,
and herd buffalo.

Some Pig!

Despite their usefulness to humans, pigs have long suffered from a bad reputation. In fact, even today people tend to think of pigs as being dirty, lazy, and unintelligent. But believe it or not, pigs are none of these.

Pigs, for example, are quite smart, and they can be taught a number of clever tricks. Pigs can learn many of the exact same tricks that people teach to dogs—sitting up, rolling over on command, and so on.

All this intelligence comes in handy when pigs are treated as pets. Their owners are constantly being surprised at how quickly pet pigs can be taught to use a litter box!

Finally, in France and Italy, pigs are trained to find a special fungus—like a mushroom—that grows underground in the wild. Called a truffle, it is a rare, expensive item that gives an unusual, earthy flavor to everything from meats to pasta. Pigs, it turns out, are expert at sniffing them out, digging them up, and even returning them uneaten to the truffle hunters.

Some people make the mistake of thinking that pigs do nothing but sleep and slop around in the mud!

Pigs are quite clever and have been known to climb right over a barnyard fence.

Life on the Farm

Pig farming in North America goes back to the 1500s and 1600s when Spanish, English, French, and other settlers brought their pigs with them to their new homes. Back then farmers and their animals usually lived together in one building. The people simply lived upstairs, and the animals lived down below! This let both the people and the animals keep warm at night.

Later, when people separated their living quarters from their animals', they still kept their pigs near the house. Why? This simply made it easier to feed the pigs kitchen scraps—the leftovers and other pieces of food left after cooking and preparing food.

Today pig farmers keep hundreds, even thousands of pigs in a clean, automated environment. The pens are cleaned, and the pigs are fed and watered each day—automatically, by sophisticated machinery. Even kitchen scraps are a thing of the past. Today's pigs live on a special diet to help them grow quickly and stay healthy.

Only the Squeal Is Left

No matter how large or small it may be, the purpose of a pig farm is to raise pigs for meat. At some point the pigs must be slaughtered and prepared for the table. The reality of this situation affects how farmers treat their animals. So, farmers treat their pigs well and sometimes even end up giving their pigs names. But they do not treat the pigs as pets, and they try not to become too attached to the animals.

When a pig is slaughtered, just about every part of the animal is used. The meat is turned into chops, roasts, bacon, and ham. The hair becomes bristles for brushes, and the skin is turned into high-quality leather. Even the pig's feet are used to make pickled pig's feet, which are considered quite a delicacy by many people.

No wonder there's an old saying that goes, "When a pig is slaughtered, only the squeal is left."

On some farms, pigs are left to wander about—and to get into whatever trouble they can find.

The Pig Sty

Most domestic animals have a home of some kind, a place in which they can get comfortable, keep out of bad weather, and be alone. For a pig, that place usually is a sty.

A pig sty is a covered pen that has a small, open run where pigs can exercise and socialize with one another. It also is the place where they are fed.

Pigs generally have an open area as well. This yard provides a place to exercise as well as a shady spot in the summer.

Pigs' outdoor area always is carefully fenced. Otherwise, pigs will dig their way out! During the summer there also is a shallow pool or pond in which the pigs can wade and stay cool.

Lying around in this muddy water is what has given pigs a reputation for being dirty. But, the truth is that the mud helps pigs protect their delicate skin from sunburn. It also helps them keep lice and other parasites away.

Except for their muddy "suntan lotion," pigs are very clean animals. For example, pigs make sure to sleep on the highest part of ground in their pen, away from the low area that they use as a toilet. This keeps the rain from washing any refuse into their bedroom!

Types of Pigs

To most people a pig is a pig. But to the people who raise them, there are many kinds of pigs. Some are large, others are small. Some are pink, while others are white or even a mixture of colors.

In the United States there are eight main types of pigs. Some are pure breeds, which means that all of their ancestors are the same type of pig. But most pigs are crossbreeds. This means that different types of pigs have mated to produce piglets of mixed breed. Most crossbreeding is done to create a pig that grows faster or weighs more or even just tastes better.

Three of the most famous breeds are the Chester White, the Yorkshire, and the Hampshire. The all-white Chester is a crossbreed of different white pigs. It originated in Chester County, Pennsylvania. The Yorkshire, another white pig, originated in England. The large, black Hampshire has a white "belt" marking. It originated in the United States.

A Colorful Cast of Characters

Among pig farmers, one of the most important characteristics for a pig to have is size. After all, the larger and heavier a pig is, the more it is worth at slaughtering time.

Today there are several breeds and varieties that are especially popular, in part because they are so big. In fact, some of them are quite huge, weighing up to 600 pounds (270 kilograms) each! Strangely enough, many of them also are interesting to look at.

The American Landrace, for example, has a long body and unusual drooping ears. Berkshire hogs are all black, while the Duroc breed is all red. The Poland China, one of the most famous pigs of all, is black with six white "points" on its face, tail, and feet. It is one of the all-time favorites of North American farmers. It has a huge appetite, matures early, and at breeding time, bears lots of little piglets. Another popular pig, the Spotted Swine, is a descendant of the Poland China. It eats even more than its ancestor, produces more baby piglets, and has even tastier meat.

Pigs come in many colors, from white to pink to spotted.

Pigs and Medicine

When it comes to animals and medical research, most people think of guinea pigs. But, strangely enough, hogs—fully grown pigs—are valuable to medical science too.

Hogs are useful mainly because their bodies' internal organs—their hearts, livers, lungs, and so on—are quite similar to those of human beings. Scientists, for example, have closely studied heart attacks in pigs because they are very similar to human heart attacks.

Beyond this, various parts of a pig can be used to treat human illnesses. Insulin, which is one of the main drugs for the treatment of diabetes, comes from pigs. Other chemicals obtained from pigs are used to treat arthritis, leukemia, and a host of other diseases.

So the next time someone you know has medical treatment, you might want to whisper a quiet "thank you" to a pig!

Vietnamese Pot-Bellied Pigs

When people want a pet pig, they rarely choose a full-size hog. Instead, they usually choose the small Vietnamese Pot-Bellied breed.

Pot-Bellied pigs, or PBPs as they are often called, originated in the Far East. And compared to enormous domestic farm pigs, PBPs are quite tiny. They average just 3 feet (91 centimeters) long and 15 inches (38 centimeters) tall, and they weigh in at only 75 to 125 pounds (34 to 56 kilograms). PBPs range in color from solid black to solid white, with a variety of spots and markings in between.

With cute, pushed-in faces and sweet personalities, PBPs are natural pets. They also are smart. They are easy to litter train, and they learn tricks quickly. Many PBPs even master the art of opening kitchen cabinets with their snouts! And any Pot-Bellied pig owner will tell you that they make much better pets than dinners!

Apartment Wanted . . . Maybe

Even small breeds of pigs, like Pot-Bellieds, are a lot of work, something people should think carefully about before they purchase or adopt one. Pigs, for example, need to exercise in the fresh air and root in the dirt with their snouts. They also need water or mud to wallow in.

All this is not to say, though, that a small pig cannot be raised indoors in a small house or apartment. A bath tub can serve as a pond. A litter box can be provided, and the pig can be trained to use it.

But if a pig is raised indoors, it must be walked outside at least once a day. This can be a problem even with as small a pig as a PBP.

When people keep pigs indoors, they must remember that, like children, pigs are clever enough to get into all kinds of trouble—and danger. Poisonous or harmful materials need to be put away, and drawers and cupboards must be closed and locked. Electrical cords need to be tucked away so the pigs can't pull appliances off the counter. Sockets even need to be covered so the pigs don't electrocute themselves.

Vietnamese Pot-Bellied pigs are an endearing pet.

Keeping a Pet Pig

For some people, Pot-Bellied pigs just aren't enough—they want a full-sized pig. Others may find an orphaned or abandoned piglet on their hands. In any event, PBPs aren't the only breed of pig kept as a pet.

Pig lovers keep piglets primarily because they are so small and cute. But in the end, of course, piglets grow up. Then their owners must either get rid of them or provide a fenced-in yard of some kind.

People have been treating their domestic pigs more or less as pets for centuries, but it has never been a very common practice. So, unlike cat and dog fanciers, pig owners have few guidebooks and owner's manuals to use.

For this reason, it is a good idea for anyone interested in keeping a pig—full-sized or miniature—to contact a nearby animal shelter that takes care of abandoned pigs. Such places can provide useful information as well as abandoned pigs to adopt. Equally important, they can give information about whether or not pigs are even allowed to be kept as pets in a particular community.

Some people just cannot resist taking on a baby pig as a pet.

Supplies and Equipment

Unlike some animals, pigs require little in the way of special equipment for their care. This is even true of household pets such as PBPs.

In general, pet pigs need no more than what people use to take care of a pet dog. This includes food and water bowls that are large and heavy enough to prevent spills. House pigs also need a leash with a harness to make walks easier. The owners of pet pigs also keep soft brushes and blankets on hand to keep the animals groomed, warm, and comfortable. It may also be necessary to trim the pig's hoofs, so having a good hoof trimming tool is important.

Most of these supplies can be obtained from a pet supply store. But it may be necessary to go to a farm supply outlet, where large-scale tools and equipment might be more common.

With a little grooming, pigs can be quite cute!

Being a Responsible Owner

Most people are surprised to learn that pigs have "big" personalities. In fact pigs often are more demanding than pet cats or dogs. A pig, for example, will follow its owner around the house or yard for hours, just looking for attention or for some kind of game to play.

Pet pigs can even be trained to walk on a leash. Special harness leashes can make walking a strong, willful pig a bit easier. But walking a pig is quite a task. Most owners say that it is more like having the pig take the person for a walk than the other way around.

A pig can live up to 20 years, and during that time it will require food, housing, trips to the vet, and grooming and other care. And when its owners go away on vacation, it will even need a pet sitter who can take care of the animal during its owners' absence. So, all in all, having a pet pig is quite a responsibility.

Pigs have big personalities and can be even more demanding than cats or dogs.

Diet and Nutrition

Regardless of whether they are kept as house pets or raised on a farm, pigs need to be fed twice a day. There is no doubt that feeding pigs is work. But it also can be great fun to watch simply because pigs enjoy eating so much.

Pigs are omnivorous, meaning that they will eat just about anything. And they often compete for their food. If there are more than two pigs, they actually will push each other out of the way in order to get to the food.

Farmers and pet owners rarely give their pigs "slop," or leftovers. Instead, they give their animals a commercial pig chow and then supplement, or add to, their diet with fresh fruits and vegetables.

Left to themselves, pigs eat a variety of roots, tubers, and leaves as well as small animals like lizards, mice, and any birds they can catch. In the farmyard, pigs are often fed in a long V-shaped trough. This gives plenty of room for all of them to eat their fill. Between feedings, pigs love an occasional apple or other healthy treat.

*Pigs enjoy an occasional apple, as well as their
normal meals of pig chow.*

*Pigs are happiest when they are poking
around looking for food.*

Handling

Whether they are farm animals or pet PBPs, pigs like to be treated kindly. For them, one of the best treats possible is to have their ears gently rubbed. Pigs are happiest, however, when they are with other pigs, poking around in the yard, digging up bugs, and eating worms.

Farmers who raise pigs understand that pigs need good treatment. In general, first-rate care produces a healthy and profitable animal. Even animals that will eventually be sold for meat need more than food, water, and a good living space.

Another part of pig care has to do with their tusks. Both male and female pigs have top canine teeth that curve upward. Their lower teeth can also grow upward and form tusks. For the safety of owners—and of other pigs—these tusks often are snipped off when the animals are still piglets. This is true of both pets and farm animals.

Health Care

On any farm the health of the animals directly influences how well the farm does financially. Sick animals are not only hard to deal with; they cost farmers money in medicine and in lost profits. For this reason, health care always is an important concern for farmers.

For pigs this means giving them clean housing and a proper diet. It also means giving them the shots and vaccines they need in order to prevent diseases. In addition, regular examinations can catch minor problems before they become major difficulties.

Pigs also need shade. Their skin is particularly sensitive, and it has little hair to protect it. A shady, watery spot is a good idea.

Experienced farmers treat most problems themselves. For many of these they can even use the same household medicines they would use on their own family members. Gauze and surgical tape take care of minor cuts and scrapes. Aloe vera gel and milk of magnesia also are tried-and-true remedies for pigs.

*Owners can handle most pig health problems
themselves, but sometimes a visit to the vet is needed.*

Pig Behavior

Pigs have many interesting behaviors. They are, for example, herd animals, which means they like to gather in groups. In the wild they may congregate in groups of 50 or more.

Pigs, of course, love to mud-bathe in order to escape the sun and heat. But even more interesting, they sometimes even build themselves crude shade shelters out of uprooted grass and mud.

Rooting in the dirt is natural behavior for pigs. In the wild they spend nearly every moment foraging for food. Domestic pigs get all the food they need from their owners. But foraging is such an important part of pigs' mental health and well-being that they continue it even when they are well fed.

Pigs also make a variety of sounds, especially during mating season or when they are searching for food. When a pig is happy, it will snort softly and sweetly. When it is unhappy, it will squeal loudly.

Rooting is natural behavior for pigs.

Getting Along with Others

Pigs are social animals, so, if possible, they should have the company of other pigs. And since they are not naturally aggressive, they can be kept with most other domesticated animals as well.

One of the few exceptions to this involves dogs. Dogs and pigs simply do not get along together. Aggressive dogs actually have been known to join together to kill small pet pigs. For this reason, the fence that keeps pet pigs in should also keep dogs out!

In contrast, pigs get along quite well with people. They will, however, try to dominate children, probably because they perceive children as smaller and weaker animals. Young children may even find themselves being pushed around by adult pigs. As a result, even the gentlest pet pigs may need to be penned when very young children are around.

Pigs are social animals who like to be with pigs and even other animals.

*Pigs sometimes need a good rest
after a hard day.*

Why Neuter Pigs?

Neutering involves minor operations that makes animals—males and females—unable to breed and reproduce. Owners of dogs and cats regularly neuter their pets. So do farmers and ranchers who produce beef cattle for the marketplace.

The owners of a pet pig might think that it is not really necessary to neuter their animal. After all, there probably are no other pet pigs in their area so it is unlikely that their pet will find a mate.

But adult male pigs, or boars, can be aggressive if they are not neutered. On top of that, they sometimes produce an unpleasant odor. Unspayed adult females (sows) have been known to be somewhat moody. As a result, experts recommend that pet pigs be neutered fairly early in their lives.

Since few people actually breed their pet pigs, the operation rarely poses problems either for owners or pets.

Here Come the Piglets

A sow is in heat (able to breed) only two or three days out of every 21 days. Gestation (how long the sow is pregnant) lasts about four months. After this, depending on the type of pig, sows will farrow, or give birth to, a litter of anywhere from six to 20 piglets.

At birth, each piglet weighs about three pounds (1.4 kilograms). But piglets grow fast. In fact, after just three weeks, piglets weigh about 10 pounds (4.5 kilograms), more than three times their birth weight!

Piglets are among the cutest of all baby animals, with funny snouts and lovely, long eyelashes. They have chubby little bodies, short legs, and lots of personality.

Baby pigs usually are kept with their mothers for eight weeks. Then they are shipped to new homes on other farms or, in the case of pets, among new families. Because pigs are such social creatures two piglets often are shipped together so they can keep each other company.

Piglets eat a lot and grow fast, going from three pounds (1.4 kilograms) to 10 pounds (4.5 kilograms) in just three weeks.

Famous Pigs

The kind and cute nature of the pig has made it an ideal subject for stories and fables. Here, in contrast to the common image of the pig as lazy and dirty, the animals are usually portrayed as smart, kind, and brave.

The most famous pigs, of course, are the ones in the old story "The Three Little Pigs." But these certainly are not the only well-known swine. From Wilbur, the lovable pig in *Charlotte's Web*, to Porky, the stuttering cartoon pig, swine have been popular figures that have amused and delighted generations of children and adults.

Some time ago television and movies introduced a major star from the pig family—the Muppet's Miss Piggy. Madly in love with herself and immensely clever, she has entertained millions of people—including the object of her affections, Kermit the Frog.

More recently the movie *Babe* added pigs to a unique form of movie magic. In it a lovable pig tries to avoid the slaughterhouse by acting like a sheepdog.

With all this, it is probably no wonder that millions of people love pigs . . . without ever having seen one close up!

Words to Know

Boar   A male hog of any age.

Crossbreeds   The offspring of two animals of different breeds, varieties, or species.

Farrow   To give birth to pigs.

Gestation   The period in which a mother carries her young; pregnancy.

Insulin   A substance that regulates the body's use of sugar.

Litter   The group of pigs a sow gives to birth to at one time.

Neuter   To remove the reproductive organs.

Omnivorous   Feeding on both plant and animal substances.

Piglet   A young, small pig.

Rooting   To dig or dig up with the snout.

Sow   A full-grown female pig.

Trough   A long, narrow, often shallow receptacle for holding water or feed for animals.

Truffle   A blackish, light-brown underground fungus used as a food and a flavoring.

INDEX

American Landrace pigs, 20
Artiodactyla, 6

Babe, 46
Berkshire pigs, 20
boar, 43
breeding, 44

Charlotte's Web, 46
Chester White pigs, 19
crossbreeds, 19

diet, 32
Duroc pigs, 20

Eurasian wild boar, 9

farrow, 44
forest hog, 9

gestation, 44

Hampshire pigs, 19
heat, 44
hogs, 22

insulin, 22

Kermit the Frog, 46
litter, 44

Miss Piggy, 46

neuter, 43

omnivorous, 32

peccary, 6
piglets, 20, 22, 44
pig sty, 18
Poland China pigs, 20
Porky, 46
pygmy hog, 9

rooting, 39

sow, 43, 44
Spotted Swine pigs, 20
Suidae, 6

teeth, 9, 35
trough, 32
truffles, 12

Vietnamese Pot-Bellied pigs
   (PBPs), 23, 24, 28

warthog, 9

Yorkshire pigs, 19

Cover Photo: Lynn M. Stone
Photo Credits: Norvia Behling (Behling & Johnson Photography), pages 14, 25, 30, 37;
Lynn M. Stone, pages 7, 11, 13, 17, 21, 26, 29, 33, 38, 41, 42; SuperStock, Inc., pages 4, 8, 34, 45.